HISTORY OF SALEM WITCH TRIALS

A BRIEF OVERVIEW FROM BEGINNING TO END

HISTORY ENCOUNTERS

History of

The Salem Witch Hunt

A Brief History from Beginning to the End

History Encounters

CONTENTS

Bonus Downloads

Want to Fill Your Digital Library for Free?

Every purchase comes with FREE bonus downloads! Download yours now by clicking the 'Get it Now' button.

Get it Now

Scan Your Phone to open QR code

Chapter One
Introduction

How do you define witches? There are so many versions of witches throughout history and literature. There are witches like the people in the Harry Potter series. But in history, these witches are nothing like the ones in Harry Potter because in Salem and in other parts of the world, it was believed that witches were the devil's worshippers. Therefore, they were seen as a cult whose purpose was to destroy Christian Society. Over multiple centuries, these fears led people to suspect and persecute witches. This period was called the Great Witch Hunts or what is more commonly known as the Burning Times.

Salem is a place founded by the Puritans, known as "extremist Protestants." This means they are Protestants from England who believe that the current religious arrangement was still too close to the Roman Catholic system. These Puritans arrived in the New World (now known as America) because they wanted a change. However, Salem wasn't the first settlement; it was actually Plymouth Colony which is near Cape Cod. Then some people thought that the changes they made religiously weren't enough, so they set off to create a new settlement in Naumkeag. This place was named, after a few years, Salem.

Now, Salem did not start right away as a place of witches. It was after a few years that it became a place where witches were persecuted. The chaos began in the household of Reverend Samuel Parris. His daughter, Elizabeth "Betty" Parris, and niece, Abigail Williams, were caught dancing in the forest with their household help, Tituba. They were suspicious of their actions, so they questioned them. Soon enough, the group of girls (it was not only Abigail and Betty in the woods with Tituba) claimed they were forced into witchcraft, being tormented by witches. And from there, the witch hunt in Salem began.

There are plenty of stories based on Salem's witch hunt. One of the stories based on it was a play written by Arthur Miller. The play is entitled "The Crucible." It was one of the most historically accurate historical fiction ever made. Arthur Miller did a lot of research to create this theatrical play. However, for drama's sake, he added some dramatic elements and removed some people involved in the stories of Salem.

Besides stories based on what transpired in Salem, there were also some documented stories on what really happened back then. The story in The Crucible is just one of many. There is one story about the hearings of Sarah Good, Sarah Osbourne, and Tituba. The story of their hearing is like what happened in The Crucible. At first, the three women denied the accusations made towards them. Still, in the end, Tituba confessed and brought the others down with her. The reason why people would take down the other accused with them is unclear to this day. However, people don't really talk about it.

Now, witch hunting's origin wasn't in Salem. It started in the Middle Ages in Europe. Since Europe was populated with Christians at that time, witch hunts began because of Bible studies. However, religion did not exactly lead to witch hunts. What really led the people of this religion to witch hunts is that the leaders at this time wanted power, and they saw this as an opportunity to gain it. They called witchcraft, back then, heresy.

As said before, the witch hunts in Salem started with Abigail Williams and the other girls in that group. However, there were more witches than just the names the girls gave. One of the key-accused of witchcraft was a reverend named George Burroughs, one of the first male witches persecuted.

As stated before, there are people in the academic world who are skeptical of the topic of witchcraft. So, they would try to find explanations – theories – as to what really happened in Salem all those years ago. Some historians, physicians, and sociologists are trying to figure out the truth. However, they still haven't come up with a conclusion until this day.

In this reading, you will read through some documented stories about what happened in Salem. You will witness the confessions, see the desperation of the accused and question the actions made by the accused. You will also see people in our time now make sense of what really happened all those years ago. Whether from a historian's or a medical expert's point of view, you will learn the different explanations they are trying to get at. It will make you ask the question: was it really witchcraft? Or was it all just ignorance?

Chapter Two

Witches and Witchcraft

Witchcraft can be defined in several ways, based on which part of history one is talking about. In some cultures, witchcraft is seen as a universally recurrent theme in most – if not all – human cultures. Other people describe witchcraft as an era in history. For skeptics, witchcraft is a made-up excuse for people to persecute their enemies.

The usual and specific definition of witchcraft is a set of rituals and behaviors that people use to perform and induce the destruction of something or someone. People believed that witches were the cause of what was truly evil in the world; since they were in close contact with the dark supernatural forces of the world.

Even though the belief is that witchcraft is used for evil, it is not automatic that those who practice it have sold their souls to the devil or worshiped demons. The people who practice witchcraft are known as witches, meaning they have also formed a cult.

Witchcraft is generally a common branch of magic. A person studying this branch of magic must have been educated in the Arcane Arts and trained in this type of magic for years. Witchcraft includes simple gestures, spells, and rituals. Also, witches were usually women who were uneducated and were part of the lowest social class.

Witchcraft itself is not inherently evil. Yes, it is known to be in contact with the damned, but that does not mean it will only be used for malicious purposes. The demons are just the source of the magic, but the way the witches use this power gives witchcraft its bad name.

People believed witches do harmful magic by getting their power from demons, which they could control through different words, signs, or gestures. To be able to get this power over demons, witches must worship them (which violates the laws of Christian Fate). Also, people thought that witches renounced their original faith to give their lives in service of Satan.

As stated earlier, witchcraft is merely a common branch of magic. Robert Thurston believed that magic could be divided into high and low. High magic can be learned only through the careful study of books. For low magic, which is where witchcraft is placed, it is innate and passed on from parent to child. Basically, high magic is learned, while low magic is something you are born with.

Thurston believed that the people who practice witchcraft (and can be prosecuted for using witchcraft) could be further categorized into three based on how these witches use the power of the devil. The first one is the usual evil witch who uses their powers for destruction. The second one is the complete opposite. The second one is called the "wise person." These people are the healers of their society. So, when the witch-hunters come knocking, the people actually defend the "wise person." Lastly, the third category comprises people who are mentally unwell. People believed these witches became mentally unstable because they forced themselves to do witchcraft – even though witchcraft is a type of magic that is inherited, not just learned.

When it comes to the beginnings of witch-hunts, there are two basic definitions in this aspect. One is that witchcraft is a sorcery that causes destruction in the world and can destroy the different religious beliefs and practices throughout many cultures and cities.

In the bible, there are different passages referring to witches, and it warns Christians of their evil. From Exodus, xii, 18: "Thou shalt not suffer a witch to live." In Leviticus, xx, 27: "A man also or a woman that hath a familiar spirit, or that is a wizard, shall surely be put to death; their blood shall be upon them." And in Deuteronomy, xviii, 9-12: Deuteronomy, xviii. 9-12: "When thou art come into the land which the Lord thy God giveth thee, thou shalt not learn to do after the abominations of those nations. There shall not be found among you anyone that maketh his son or his daughter to pass through the fire, or that useth divination, or an observer of times, or any enchanter, or a witch, or a charmer, or a consulter with familiar spirits, or a wizard, or a necromancer; for all that do these things are an abomination unto the Lord."

Thanks to Mr. Ward of New England, who followed the teachings of Moses (the one who gave the ten commandments to man), this is why there is the persecution of witches. Death is the only punishment for witches.

Chapter Three

Salem

Salem was where the Puritans (who are basically like Extremist Protestants) settled during the Reformation in England. They were men and women who were not exactly criminals or tyrannical people, but they were rebels. They are rebels because they cannot respect the forced religious rituals their country, England, is making them do. Salem became their safe haven, their "castle on a cloud." Salem has become their safe house.

But, of course, the people did not discover Salem right away. The first people to come to the New World made their settlement in Plymouth Colony, near Cape Cod. Although this may be a "safe place" for the Puritans, some believed that the people living in Plymouth Colony weren't as separated from the Church of England as they'd liked. So a group of them, including John Lyford, set off to find another settlement where the severed ties from the Church of England are cut straight through.

The first settled in Nantasket but quickly moved to Cape Ann. They established their village as a farming and fishing community. Roger Conant soon joined their little community and quickly became Governor. However, soon they saw that fishing and farming had become unfruitful work. There was no profit in it anymore. So, Conant brought everyone to Naumkeag and made a whole new settlement there.

After a few years, the Massachusetts Bay Colony saw that Naumkeag was struggling. Even though the settlers in Naumkeag had grit, keeping their relatively new settlement up and afloat was hard.

Because, again, of the Reformation and what was happening in the New World, a group of people in England banded together to create the "Governor and Colony of Massachusetts Bay in New England." John Endicott was appointed Governor. Endicott, his wife, and some followers sailed to the New World around June 1628. They arrived in early September. In April, the other people from England left their country to join the colony in America. Therefore, they brought in more resources from England.

John Endicott, being the Governor of the new society mentioned earlier, brought in resources to Naumkeag to help build up the town more. However, besides good fortunes, he brought in his own grit and wanted to take over Naumkeag. Without much of a fight, Conant gave Endicott the reins to Naumkeag. Because of his peacefulness, Endicott gave Conant a big plot of land to stay in happily until the end of his days. Thankful for a peaceful transition, Naumkeag was renamed "Salem."

At the start of Salem's history, the men of this town decided not to bring any church with them. Instead, they all decided to make one, so it will be independent of all other churches. There was a meeting about this on July 20, 1629. Ultimately, it was agreed upon that Skelton was the Pastor, and Higginson was the appointed teacher. The nine deacons and ruling elders were also delegated to the other people. So, on that day, the First Church at Salem was also the first Protestant Church in America.

When Endicott and Conant started to work together, the town of Salem thrived in more ways than one. By 1636, they had their first trade ship sailed to the West Indies. In 1644, the first fort in Salem's built, establishing itself as a strong Massachusetts town. There were other buildings coming in, such as the Custom House, the House of the Seven Gables, and the Witch House.

However, even though Salem seemed to be buzzing with new and good energy, they were still not politically stable. This is so because of the chaos happening in England (Protestants Vs. Everyone else). Because of all of that, there was a nine-year war known as King William's War. It made life for the people of Salem quite difficult.

If we look more closely, Salem may have been buzzing in a good way macroscopically. But if you look closer, Salem was not as stable as most people would think. Once Conant and Endicott's days ended, Salem was split into two: Salem Town. The other one is called Salem Village, where the residents are stubborn and aggressive. Salem Village is where most – if not all – witch hunts and trials were done.

Before the witchcraft time of Salem, the Puritan's patience for intolerance has been strong throughout the years. The Brownes were sent back to England for opposing Endicott and the First Church. Endicott destroyed the red cross from the flag because it reminded him of the Christian Pope symbol. Roger Williams was banished for preaching something other than Puritan teachings. And those are just the tip of the iceberg.

This is a picture of a witch from Salem.

Chapter Four

The Start of Witches in Salem

The accusations of witches in New England were uncommon since they started in the 1630s, primarily around the colonies of Massachusetts Bay and Connecticut. The people of Salem began to become suspicious of witchcraft in their houses because of what happened underneath the roof of Reverend Samuel Parris. Samuel Parris is the pastor of the church at Salem Village.

Elizabeth Parris, Abigail Williams, and Tituba used to assemble together inside the minister's kitchen to experiment with incantations. Among these three girls are Ann Putnam, Mercy Lewis, Elizabeth Hubbard, and Sarah Churchill. Among the things they've done are: palmistry and other arts of fortune-telling, reading up on necromancy, magic, and spiritualism.

Someone then noticed their strange behavior: going into holes, creeping under the chairs, having little ticks and gestures, and even muttering weird words. Soon enough, more people noticed all these, including the elders. They sent for Dr. Griggs to treat them. However, he cannot figure out what is wrong with the girls. According to Dr. Griggs, what they had was unheard of in the field of science. Forced to be able to give a diagnosis, Dr. Griggs said that the devil possessed the girls. And because of this, the whole village got curious and alarmed. People would approach the house and observe the strange mannerisms of the girls.

Mr. Parris finally took matters into his own hands. He requested a meeting with the other parishes to help him with his predicament. He called upon them to pray and investigate his daughter and the other girls. In the end, they all agree with Dr. Griggs; the girls are possessed. It was common back then that doctors would pin the blame of the unknown on the devil.

Now, all the questions are pouring out. Who did this to the girls? Why did they do it? How can they heal them of this bewitchment? Mr. Parris and some other people took it upon themselves to get to the bottom of this problem.

Tituba, the house help of the Parris family, was accused of being a witch herself and is one of the reasons why this is happening to the other girls. She, according to others, is the origin of Salem's witchcraft. Tituba came from New Spain, more commonly known as the Spanish West Indies. They believe d that she brought in her native practices, which could be suspected of witchcraft.

Elizabeth Parris, who is suspected of being the leader in this group at the start of everything, was sent away by her father to the family of Stephen Sewall for her own protection. Abigail Williams, the niece of Mr. Parris, seemed to be drawn to the witchcraft arts from the beginning all the way to the end. Ann Putnam, the daughter of Sergeant Thomas Putnam, was seen to be the leader of the whole group throughout all the mischief they've caused. Mary Walcot, the daughter of Jonathan Walcot, and Mercy Lewis, who lived with the Burroughs family, were also a part of this group. Elizabeth Hubbard was the niece of Dr. Griggs; she was also a part of this group.

Beyond the young girls, there were other people who were afflicted with the same afflictions. Sarah Good and Sarah Warren-Osbourne are two women who fit the profile of those who were accused of witchcraft.

Among all the ones who people were suspicious of, only three were convicted. They were Tituba, Sarah Good, and Sarah Osbourne. After their arrest, they were sent to two judges in Salem Town. The judges were: John Hathorne and Jonathan Corwin. After their trial, Good and Osbourne were said to be innocent, while Tituba was found guilty. Tituba was then put up for interrogation.

As the magistrates questioned Tituba, she first denied hurting all the young women. She confessed, however, that "the devil came to me and bid me to serve him." Still, she denies all accusations about inflicting harm on the girls. However, Judge Hathorne pushed on until she eventually gave up and conceded. However, she didn't go down without a fight. She brought down Good and Osbourne with her. But she also stated that a man from Boston helped inflict pain on the other women.

And because of all this, the Salem Witch Hunt just carried on. When they heard about Tituba's confession, the people in Salem Village were all affected. Tituba stated that around seven more people were practicing witchcraft in their midst, and it scared them all.

And so, the hunt continues.

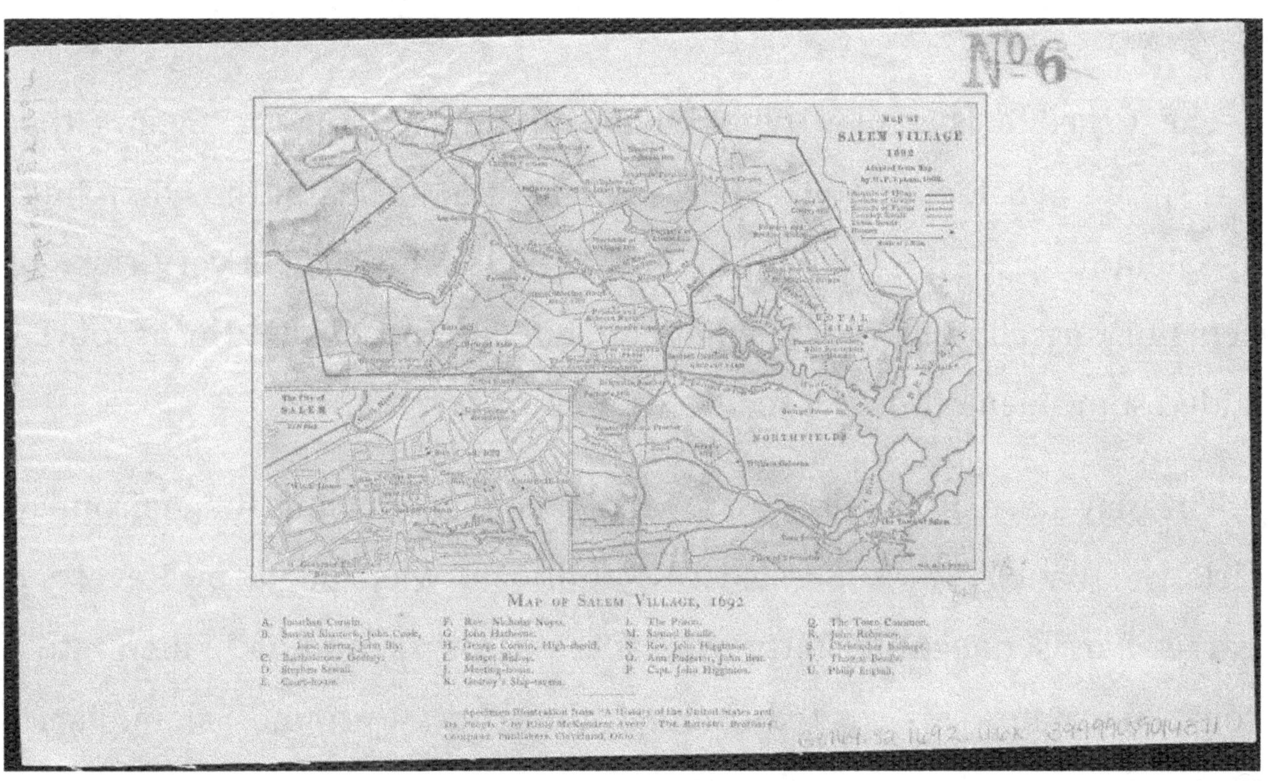

This is the map of Salem.

Chapter Five

The Crucible

The Crucible is a play by Arthur Miller based on the events that transpired in Salem in 1692. He researched the events of the witch hunt in Salem to write this play in the early 1950s. This play is very close to being historically accurate to what happened in those days. He, of course, added some elements for it to be a dramatic play.

The play starts in the Puritan town of Salem, Massachusetts. A group of girls was dancing in a forest with Tituba and was caught by Reverend Parris. Parris' daughter, Betty, was one of the girls and had fallen into a coma-like state. This started rumors of witchcraft around Salem. Parris requested that Reverend John Hale come because of his experience with witchcraft. Parris also interrogates his niece, Abigail Williams (who is part of the group of girls), about what happened in the forest. Abigail just said that they were dancing and nothing else.

Parris then comes out to the crowd, gathering by his home to calm them down. While this is happening, Abigail talks to the other girls, forcing them not to speak about what really happened in the forest. John Proctor, a farmer, comes in to talk to Abigail alone. Most people don't know of their affair with each other when Proctor is working in their home. However, Abigail still wants Proctor, but he denies her every single time.

In the next scene, Betty wakes up screaming. People rushed upstairs, curious as to what was happening. Then Proctor, Parris, Giles Corey, and Thomas Putnam have an argument about money and land deeds. Reverend Hale then enters to examine Betty and questions Abigail about what happened in the forest. He is unconvinced about her story and demands to have a chat with Tituba.

After Parris and Hale question Tituba, she confesses to conspiring with the devil and blames the people of Salem, who also are consorting with the devil. Abigail confirms her accusation, saying she's also seen people conversing with the devil. Betty also joins in, giving names to the witches in Salem.

After a week, John and Elizabeth Proctor were talking about the ongoing trials in their own home. Elizabeth pleads with John to reveal Abigail as a fraud, but he doesn't want to. Then his wife becomes jealous, accusing him of still having feelings for Abigail. Then Mary Warren, their servant who is also part of Abigail's circle, comes in with news that Elizabeth is being accused of witchcraft. Still, the court decided not to push through with this accusation. They made Mary go to bed to continue their conversation. But they were interrupted by Reverend Hale. Then Giles Corey and Francis Nurse come in to say that their own wives have been arrested. After that, people came in to arrest Elizabeth. John rushed to Mary, telling her to go to Salem and reveal Abigail and the other girls as frauds.

The next day, John brings Mary to court and forces her to testify against the other girls. Judge Danforth is suspicious of John's actions and reveals that Elizabeth is actually pregnant so that she will be spared for the time being. But John insists that Danforth should allow Mary to say that the girls are lying. Then the girls are summoned to court, and they claim that Mary is actually bewitching them. John grows angry and admits his affair with Abigail, saying that her desire for him is the reason behind her accusations. She's just jealous of his wife. To test John's accusation, Danforth brings in Elizabeth and asks her if John has cheated on her. However, even though she knows the truth, she lies to protect John's reputation. So the judge says that John is a liar. After that, Abigail and the other girls start to spasm out of control, claiming that Mary is tormenting them. Mary, distressed, accuses John of being a witch. John is enraged, but he's quickly arrested, and Hale stops the hearing.

Seasons change, and the witch trials have caused a strain in the neighboring towns of Salem. Danforth is nervous, and Abigail has run away with all her uncle's money. Hale has lost faith in the justice system. However, he gets an idea. He requests Elizabeth to talk to John to confess that he is a witch, and Elizabeth agrees to this plan. John is persuaded to do so. However, he was asked to give more names of possible witches in court. He doesn't, though, and the court states that he should confess in public then. John grows angry and retracts his statement. Then John was sent to the gallows, which is when the play ends.

Chapter Six

The Hearing of Sarah Good and Sarah Osbourne

We've established that the three main suspects were Tituba, Sarah Good, and Sarah Osbourne. They tormented the group of young girls. They all had the template to be witches. Sarah Good was in her late thirties, poor and isolated. Even her own husband thought she was guilty of being a witch. She would speak under her breath when people annoyed her. She was the epitome of a scorned woman. For Sarah Osbourne, her template was that she was outcast for living with another man after her husband died and for skipping mass for more than a year. As for Tituba, she was an Indian slave, and as a woman, she was difficult. So yes, these three girls were the perfect examples of witches.

On leap day, the people asked for Law Enforcement to step in. The people wanted the women to be brought to court and face justice. They demanded a pretrial hearing. Even though this meant that they wouldn't be sentenced just yet, the people believed this would bring up any evidence of other witches living among them.

Jonathan Corwin and John Hathorne were the judges in this hearing. Bartholomew Gedney joined in with them. In the hearing, they thought it best to bring in the girls who accused Sarah Good, Sarah Osbourne, and Tituba. The accusers Elizabeth "Betty" Parris, Abigail Williams, Ann Putnam, and Elizabeth Hubbard came to the hearing.

At this point, all of Salem were aware of the situation. They know of what transpired in the house of Reverend Parris. They know of the accused and what they are accused of. People from the village all came to the hearing.

During the hearing, Sarah Good denied all the accusations towards her. When she did this, the group of young girls went into a frenzy, as if they were being possessed and tormented. Being in such close proximity created a scene—the young girls spasming and seizing in front of the judges and the rest of the village. Everyone looked at the accused witches with horror and judgment. In a frenzy, the judges tried to communicate with the girls, but to no avail.

Sarah Good then finally accused Sarah Osbourne as the witch behind everything. After she said that, the young girls suddenly went back to normal. Even though this accusation seemed to save the girls, Sarah Good had too many enemies now for her to be cleared of all charges.

When Sarah Osbourne went into the spotlight, the young girls said the same thing about her as they did to Sarah Good. They said that they were hurt and tortured by her hand. They also said that she watched as they were assaulted. Sarah Osbourne, just like Sarah Good, denied all these accusations.

An actress playing "Mary" in the staged play "The Crucible."

Bonus Download

Want to Fill Your Digital Library for Free?

Every purchase comes with FREE bonus downloads! Download yours now by clicking the 'Get it Now' button.

Get it Now

Scan Your Phone to open QR code

Chapter Seven

Tituba's Confession

Tituba, an Indian slave, at first denied all accusations against her. However, in the end, she confessed. She played it smart, realizing that denying would add fuel to the flames. She thought that saying she did it would make her seem cooperative rather than crazy, like Sarah Good and Sarah Osbourne.

She admitted that the devil asked her to serve him. She also said that Sarah Good and Sarah Osbourne were her accomplices. Tituba claimed that she saw a "tall man" in Boston the night before and that the man made her harm the young girls. Then she apologized for all the trouble she caused the village, especially Abigail Williams and the other young girls.

The judges saw the opportunity to use this situation to their advantage. They used Tituba to learn more about the devil and his plans.

The questions moved away from her crimes to her experiences of serving evil. Tituba explained that the devil came to her in the form of a hog and a giant black dog and promised her a whole lot of treasures if she served him. She recounted when the "tall man" forced her into hurting the girls and how they came to her just before she went to sleep.

During the second day of her trial, Tituba said that the devil said he was a god and made her serve him for six years, and she had to sign her name on the devil's book. The judges saw this as another opportunity to learn more about this. They knew Tituba couldn't read, but they asked anyway if she was able to see other names in the book. She said she didn't see the names but knew that Sarah Good and Sarah Osbourne's names were there. She also revealed that there were nine other names in total.

Because of Tituba's confession, the mass Salem Witch Hunt started.

Chapter Eight

The Church of Salem

The Church greatly influenced Salem at that time. With witchcraft becoming rampant, the ministers of the Church would use their sermons to preach its evil and urge people to reconnect with their Christian faith.

There was a book entitled "Malleus Maleficarum" (in English, it translates to "the Hammer of Witches"). It was written by Heinrich Kramer and James Sprenger. This book was the most-read book of that time. Of course, that's after the Bible. The book is about witches and how people can recognize their actions. It is about how to get a confession out of them and the consequences of their actions. However, the book only gave a one-sided mindset of this whole situation. It said that everything that isn't within the teachings of the Church is evil, and the devil is behind it. This book, at that time, was used as a guide for witch-hunters.

Samuel Parris is a minister of the Church of Salem. He was the epitome of greed back in the day. He seems like he wants what is best for the parishioners when in truth, he just wants to acquire more wealth for himself. He uses religion to hide the fact that he is getting the fruits of other people's labor. He is accustomed to a certain high standard of living. This is shown in the fact that he had two Indian slaves in his household when he moved to Salem with his daughter.

Samuel Parris suspected witchcraft in Salem when his daughter Elizabeth fell ill with an unexplainable disease. According to the play, "The Crucible" by Arthur Miller, this happened after she and Abigail Williams, her cousin, joined in on a black magic ritual with Tituba. Historically speaking; however, she became ill after they tried to get to know their future husbands. However, as it is obvious, their ceremony went terribly wrong.

Because of this, for sure, Parris knew about the inner workings of witchcraft since it was not only happening under his roof but also because the Church studied the topic. The ministers thought it best to learn this so that they know of the dangers it can bring to their Church and their belief in God.

Reverend John Hale is another important person in the Church of Salem at the time of witches. However, he was not from Salem Village. He was called upon to the village because of his experience with exorcism and demonology. He's also not a stranger to witch trials and interrogations of the accused people. John Hale was an avid believer in witchcraft. However, he became a bit skeptical of it when his own wife was accused of being a witch.

In "The Crucible," he was described as a man who believed in witchcraft, and his faith greatly influenced his actions in God. Therefore, he had no ulterior motives like Samuel Parris. Like the others, he believed that he must study witchcraft to defend everyone's Christian faith, or else the devil would rule them. This is why he accepts the request for him to go to Salem.

This is a picture of Reverend Samuel Parris.

Chapter Nine

Origins of Witch Hunting

Witch hunting started out in the Middle Ages. Although most societies are divided in political matters, Christianity is what united the people. This community is called "Christendom." This community ended paganism in their land. Christian leaders insisted on their belief to be everyone's, except for the Jews and Muslims, who were allowed to live within the borders of Christendom.

Christianity, surprisingly, did not lead to witch-hunting because of the divide in the Middle Ages. For Western Europe, the pope slowly was able to acquire power, administrative and spiritual, over the Christian Church. After some time, the Christians of Eastern Rome (also known as the Byzantine Empire) fought back their rise to power. This caused a split between the two regions of Christendom. They were divided into two branches now: Catholics in the west and Orthodox in the east. However, they still shared many beliefs and practices.

For witchcraft, however, they were still divided. The Orthodox Church never gained interest in demonology or strixology (the study of witches and witchcraft). This is so because they believed the Christian faith does not need to fear the supernatural.

However, in the rest of Europe, theologians had a discussion about the existence of demons. Towards the end of the Middle Ages, the pagan influences of Greece and Rome, heresies, and the concern towards demons caused the people to build the gallows for witches. When the political system got involved, witches suffered even more.

A medieval explanation for the rise of heretics at that time was that the devil was to blame for everything. The people in power accused the heretics of consorting with the devil and denying God. They said they formed demonic promises and did sinful acts. These charges soon became the same for witches.

Heresy then became synonymous with the dark side of the supernatural. Therefore, they've become synonymous with witches as well. One of the first records of heresy was in France in 1022. King Robert II of France sentenced a group of heretics who were accused of conjuring demons and other demonic actions. The sentence was to burn them alive in a cottage.

Another example was when Abbot Guibert of Nogent questioned heretics in Soissons in the early twelfth century. He was familiar enough with heresy to be able to identify heretics. However, he wasn't able to gain answers to his questions. So, they used water to get a response. If they float, they are guilty.

There are other stories of witches and magic at this time. However, there was little documentation on it. The Church leaders had three ways to solve this mass outbreak of heresy. The first is the Mendicant Orders. This method established a passive way to clear heretics. They would preach to the common people, converting heretics back to Christianity. The second method was the crusades, where they dealt with heretics in a violent way. The last method was through the Inquisition. In this method, they used politics to stop the heretics. This is where the hunts and trials began.

The Inquisition has five phases. The first phase is for the people to report heresy to the tribunal. The second phase is where they summon the accused and the witnesses. The third phase requires the inquisitors to examine the claims. During this phase, the accused would stay in a jail cell. The inquisitors may torture the accused if they see fit. The goal of this phase is to get a confession. The fourth phase is a trial, which is often quick. During this trial, the accused are at a disadvantage. They had no right to legal representation and no right to challenge any evidence against them. The final phase is when the tribunal gives a verdict. If they deem the accused not guilty, they will be set free. But if they see the accused as guilty, they would force them to repent and reconcile. The punishment won't be as harsh if the accused admits their guilt.

Chapter Ten

Theories about the Witch Hunts in Europe

People have been looking for explanations for the witch hunts. Historians steer away from supernatural explanations as they go down the anthropological path of explaining the witch hunts. They don't bother to answer the question of whether magic is real or not. They only want to answer the question of whether people back then really believed in magic or not.

Some modern historians believe that witches are real, and so are their powers. Historians such as Jules Michelet and Montague Summers take the confessions of the past quite seriously. They believed these people really did torture the devil and practiced the dark arts. Around the 1920a, Margaret Murray believed that the witches were actually pagans who worshiped the god Janus. Her theory was later on named "Murrayite Theory."

Though, some historians don't believe that there were pagans in western Europe in the 19th century because these practices were either phased out or absorbed into the Christian framework.

There are other historical theories that focus on the people who persecuted the witches. Some, like George Lincoln Burr and Henry Charles Lea, believed that the desire for money and power motivated the hunts. They thought the Church made up the stories of witches to be able to gain power and wealth and strengthen the Christian Church.

Many of the scholars did see a similarity between the accused witches. Most of them were part of lower society and were extremely poor. Other historians even believed that conflict between the Protestants and Roman Catholics was what started and catalyzed the hunts for witches. This is so because they think the devil wanted to tear the Church apart by causing this chasm between the two religions.

Besides historical theories, there are scientific theories as well. Scientists believed this whole debacle was because of an unidentifiable illness back then. They would think the disease must be caused by an infection, poison, or hallucinogenic drugs. For them, this is a solid reason for the idea of witches.

Psychologists have several explanations for the idea of witches and the hunts. However, this does not mean they've reached a consensus on the affliction. Some of them think it was caused by "culture-bound syndromes" or "mass sociogenic hysteria." Some Freudians believe all demons and the devil are a projection of one's superego and ego. In some cases, possession can be explained by dissociation (splitting of a person's personality). Sadly, these theories can never be tested because all the would-have-been patients are dead.

There are also some sociological theories regarding this topic. Some historians would think the rise of power in the national governments is directly related to the development of witch hunts. All people in power were focused on increasing their control over the people. Scholars believed these power-hungry men saw witchcraft as a threat to their rise. As a result, they antagonized witchcraft and started witch hunts. They did everything in their power to protect their climb to power. Theories regarding social functionalism or social accusation were enough for the historians of sociology to explain the witch hunts.

This is the Funeral Plaque of John Proctor.

Chapter Eleven

Witch Hunt in Salem

In May of 1692, the Massachusetts governor, Sir William Phipps, created a court specifically for witchcraft cases. He appointed nine people to be part of this court. The head of this court is lieutenant governor William Stoughton.

The court convened a meeting in early June and sentenced the first witch to be hanged. However, their decision seemed like it needed to be explained to the public. Cotton Mather drafted their statement, acknowledging the gravity of what had been happening. Mather also mentioned that the system by which they convict suspects is based on spectral evidence and other kinds of baseless statements.

George Burroughs was the person behind all the demonic happenings – and he's a reverend. He grew up in Maryland and graduated from Harvard, missing by a narrow margin Samuel Parris. He arrived at Salem Village in his late twenties; he stayed for three years. When he returned, he terrorized Salem Village. His first hunt was the daughter of Parris, who he choked to death. He murdered several more women and some French and Indian people. He was a man with a mission: to teach children how to fear God. He was the one who supervised the Satanic Sabbaths.

When it came to Burrough's preliminary hearing, a lot of people testified. Eight people confessed to being a witch and claimed he was promised a throne on Satan's side. The girls showed scars and marks on their skins that were put there by Burrough. For the people who he choked, the judges had to wait until the people had recovered.

Chief Justice Stoughton was confused as to the appearance of ghosts. They knew they weren't hallucinating because others who weren't bewitched could see them too. One girl, however, screamed, claiming that she could see the bloody faces of Burrough's dead wives. These ghosts wanted justice for their lives.

Sort of desperate, Burroughs got a piece of paper from his pocket and read from it. He said, "there neither are nor ever were witches, that having made a compact with the Devil can send a Devil to torment other people at a distance." This caused trouble because if witchcraft didn't exist, and if the devil didn't make anyone do anything, the tribunal had already sentenced six innocent people to death.

However, Stoughton saw the piece of paper and recognized it from the work of Thomas Ady. Thomas Ady is a skeptical man who doesn't believe in witches. Instead, he believes ignorant doctors caused this whole trouble. Burroughs, of course, lied about getting this from Ady's works.

On the morning of August 19, the first men who were from Massachusetts were to be executed. The people accused were: George Burroughs, George Jacobs, John Proctor, and John Willard. However, they still claimed to be innocent and were hopeful the true witches would come and be revealed. Even as they stared at the face of death, they forgave their accusers, the justice system, and the jury. They were still optimistic that they'd be pardoned in the minutes before their execution. But that didn't happen, and they all died.

This is the Funeral Plaque of George Burroughs.

Chapter Twelve

Events in Salem Explained

There are several theories about what really happened in Salem at the time of the witch-hunt. The oldest being that there was mass deception and fraud. Some people back then believed in the explanation by Robert Calef and Thomas Brattle, who blamed Cotton Mather for defending the justice system and supporting all the accusers.

Later on, in the nineteenth century, a man named Charles Upham gathered documentation and testimonies and wrote his opinion into a book entitled "Salem Witchcraft." Another book for readers who want answers was "The Devil in Massachusetts," written by Marion Starkey. And, of course, another documentation of what happened back then that is still important until now is Arthur Miller's "The Crucible."

In 1969, Chadwick Hansen wrote a book entitled "Witchcraft at Salem" where he expressed his opinions on what happened. In his book, he states that Upham's views are wrong. Hansen meticulously read all testimonies and decided there were indeed witches in Salem.

After a few years, a man named Keith Thomas wrote a book entitled "Religion and the Decline of Magic." Even though his book is based on the events in England and not in Salem, his words sparked some historians to a template for what he said. They used it to analyze Salem's misfortune. Thomas said that there were a lot of folk stories and that the people accused had similarities. He also was the one to point out that the art of magic changes over time.

Even though some historians are a bit doubtful of Thomas' work, he still was able to create a new outlook on the events in Salem. He showed that Salem is actually a bad example of American Puritanism.

Around 1970, many more historians took an interest in the witchcraft events in Salem. Two historians were able to give a new perspective on what happened in Salem. They were Paul Boyer and Stephen Nissenbaum, and they wrote a book called "Salem Possessed." They explained the feud between the Putnams and Porters. It described the witchcraft cases that had some English practices in them.

Around the 1980s, a historian named Carol Karlsen wrote: "The Devil in the Shape of a Woman," which comprised statistical information. It showed that most people who were accused of witchcraft were women. She said that the accused were mostly older women who weren't thriving as much as the others.

Some medical researchers also tried to explain the events of Salem. For example, there is one theory that says people ate spoiled wheat. This means that what they ate made them go temporarily mad, causing them to hallucinate and spasm out of control. The scientists and historians tried to look at the vents together and agreed that history might be wrong. They think there must have been an external factor.

After much research, it is obvious there is still a lot of speculation and doubt about what really happened. There is no set explanation that could be said. However, there are still some people: historians, doctors, and other scholars, who are trying to uncover the truth of the Salem witch hunt and trials.

Pictured above is the memorial for the victims of the Salem Witch Trials.

Chapter Thirteen

Conclusion

Surely, after reading this, you have so many questions. And to be honest, you might not get answers to most of them. For example, you may be wondering why the accused, who have accepted the accusations towards them, would bring down other people by saying they are witches. Or is witchcraft real, or was it just some ploy for some people to gain more power? The truth is, because it is history, we won't be able to answer these questions accurately. Everything at this point is speculation and opinions.

The events that transpired in Salem at that time are factual, yes. However, it may only be factual then but not now. History can be tricky. Some parts of it are sincerely hard facts like war. But there are others, like this topic, that are subject to study further because the problem back then, which was witchcraft, is not real to this day - unlike war. On the news, we no longer hear that "a witch has been convicted of murder." Though there are some who are into witchcraft, even then, people are skeptical about it. The main problem then was witchcraft, which does not exist today. So, this opens up a lot of questions and very few answers.

Something you should have learned, however, is that history can be seen from different perspectives. This is so because history is a story where there is more than just one side of it. If we were to learn history from just one account, we would not learn and become ignorant.

What happened in Salem can be seen from different perspectives. One could be from the perspective of a bystander, another from the eyes of the church, and another view from the accused. Learning to understand all sides of a story can help you make a better conclusion and informed opinions. Accounts always have different perspectives, and we must learn to know them all.

For instance, if you've only read the account of the researchers that witchcraft was just a way for the people in power to gain more control for themselves, you will never completely understand why people actually believed in witchcraft. The happenings in Salem have many explanations. You must read all of them to be able to agree or disagree with them.

Another lesson you must keep with you is that discrimination can be found anywhere. It would be best if you never did it because it is wrong and will always have dire consequences. If you remember from the reading, you will see that it is mentioned that accused witches have a sort of pattern in them. They are usually women of a lower class. Because of this, it is possible that these women were wrongfully accused just because of their status in life. Discrimination is never good, and you must always stay away from it.

In summary, you should keep with you after reading this that you must always be familiar with the different points of view when it comes to history so you will learn and make informed opinions. And it would be best if you also remembered to avoid discrimination because of its innate wrongness and horrible consequences.

Chapter Fourteen

"Discuss with Friends and Family"

Discussion Question

In some texts, historians believed that witchcraft was the excuse for the people in power to gain more power. But some medical professionals believe it was a disease doctors back then were too ignorant to identify. Which theory do you believe in? Or do you have a theory about it yourself?

Discussion Question

Witchcraft was thought to be evil, and the people who practice it are evil. Do you think that witchcraft is evil? Or was it made evil by the people who practiced it?

Discussion Question

Some witches, like Tituba, admitted that they were witches while bringing other people down with them. For Tituba, she brought down Sarah Good and Sarah Osbourne. Why do you think they did this?

Discussion Question

Some studies show that the accused were usually lonely women of a lower social class. This could be seen as discrimination. However, why do you think people thought women like these were witches? What about them made people discriminate against them?

Discussion Question

Let's say that witchcraft is real and you were part of the tribunal.

There was a hearing, and the accused was proven guilty. Do you think

execution is the best sentence for a proven witch?

Discussion Question

Witches are known to be the devil's worshippers. They say they worship him because of his promises to them, like he would give them riches and prosperity. If you were contacted by the devil and given the same deal, would you do it? Why or why not?

Discussion Question

Witchcraft was known to draw its source for demon energy back then; therefore, it is considered evil. However, how could you persuade the witches to use this kind of magic for the good of others instead? Do you think it's possible to do this?

Discussion Question

Some people think that witnesses are enough to convict someone of being a witch. Do you think this is enough evidence to make you convinced she's guilty? Or is there a specific type of evidence you want to be given to you before you make a decision?

Chapter Fifteen

"Test Your Knowledge"

Quiz Question

1. **True or False:** Witchcraft is a low kind of magic. This means that one can practice witchcraft just by studying it. It is also known to be demonic in nature.

2. **True or False:** Salem is a place founded by the Puritans. They think of this as their safe haven. Also, this town was not crawling with witches when the Puritans first founded it.

3. **True or False:** The Crucible is a movie written by Arthur Miller. The story was based on what happened in Salem during the time of witches. It revolves around the situation of John Proctor.

4. **True or False:** Sarah Good's daughter and Sarah Osbourne's son were accused of witchcraft along with Tituba. Their children denied being witches however, when Tituba confessed, she brought them down with her. In the end, all three of them were found guilty.

5. **True or False:** The Church had great influence over the town of Salem. When the witch hunt began, they preached Christian beliefs, hoping that the people straying away from God would return. The

town of Salem called on Reverend John Hale to help them in this crisis because of his knowledge and experience with demonology and exorcism.

6. **True or False:** The concept of Witch Hunts started in the Ice Age. It died, but then it came back during the Middle Ages. The crusades were a way for them to eradicate paganism, including witchcraft.

7. **True or False:** In the Middle Ages, witchcraft was synonymous with heresy. There were three ways they tried to eradicate it. One of them was the crusades.

8. **True or False:** The historians believed that witchcraft was a way for the people of the church to gain power. The psychologists believe witches were actually sick with mental illnesses that cause hallucinations. Both of these views are still debated today.

Quiz Answer

1. False. Since it is categorized as a form of low magic, it can only be done by people who have it passed down to them by their parents AND studied.

2. True

3. False. The Crucible was written as a theatrical play, not a movie.

4. False. It was Sarah Good and Sarah Osbourne themselves who were accused of witchcraft.

5. True

6. False. The origins of Witch Hunting date back to the Middle Ages.

7. True

8. True

Bonus Download

Want to Fill Your Digital Library for Free?

Every purchase comes with FREE bonus downloads! Download yours now by clicking the 'Get it Now' button.

Get it Now

Scan Your Phone to open QR code

Final Words From the Author...

Dear Reader,

It was my utmost privilege performing a deep dive to bringing this book for you today.

Before saying goodbye, I'd like to take opportunity to offer you one final gift. If you've enjoyed this book, may I ask for a small review?

If you do, I'll send you for FREE a most cherished and valuable gift as a way of showing my utmost appreciation:

Bestsellers Top 7 Treasure Box

These are my personal bestsellers sold at bookstores valued at ~$30USD, my gift to you absolutely FREE.

To claim your gift:

1. Leave a review where the book was purchased
2. Send a screenshot to irvinepress@mail.com
3. Receive your gift of **Bestsellers Top 7 Treasure Box**

Sincerely,

History Encounters

THANK YOU